75+1=FUN

Learning Games for Children

by Donna Skinner

STANDARD PUBLISHING
Cincinnati, Ohio   2799

ISBN: 0-87239-445-X

Table of Contents

* little or no preparation

Game 1. Bible Verse Relay (Age 7-12)

You will need:

Four brightly wrapped boxes, direction cards, two Bibles, sentence strips, two magic markers

Preparation:

1. Make a set of direction cards. *(Hop three times on your right foot. Touch your nose with your right hand. Tap your forehead twice with your right hand and once with your left hand, etc.)*
2. Write Bible verses on sentence strips. Leave out one or two words but insert a blank line for the word.
3. Place two boxes containing the directions at the starting line.
4. Place two boxes containing the sentence strips about halfway across the room.
5. Place two open Bibles and two magic markers on a table at the finish line.

How to play:

1. Divide the children into two teams.
2. At the call of "Go," the leaders pick a direction card from the first box, and perform the activity.
3. Then each child races to the second box and picks up a sentence strip.
4. Next, they race to the table, look up the Scripture, and write the correct word in the blank with the magic marker.
5. They return the sentence strip to the teacher. The second child on the team picks a direction card from the box and begins.
6. The team that finishes first wins the game.
7. Be sure to read the Bible verses aloud when the game is finished.

Game 2. We're Marching to Jerusalem (Age 7-9)

You will need:

Record player

Preparation:

Place enough chairs in a circle for all the children.

How to play:

1. Seat the children in a circle.
2. Start the music.
3. Remove one chair each time the music starts.
4. Children march around in a circle chanting, "We're marching to Jerusalem!"
5. All the children try to sit down when the music stops. Each time one child is eliminated.
6. The last child in the game is the winner.

Game 3. Catch-a-Pie (Age 4-7)

You will need:

Paper plate or pie tin, pictures of eye, ear, nose, mouth, and hands, glue, magic marker, scissors

Preparation:

1. Divide the pie plate into five pieces with the magic marker.
2. Paste one of the pictures on each of the pie divisions.

How to play:

1. All of the children sit in a circle.
2. One person is chosen to be "It."
3. "It" spins the plate and calls out a name.
4. The child whose name is called must stop the plate while it is still spinning.

5. He must then name the function of the body part his hand is touching.
6. The next person who spins that body part must name a different function.
7. If the child can't name the function, or renames a function already used in the game, he is out.
8. The last person left in the game is the winner.

Game 4. Jesus Gave Me (Age 6-10)

You will need:

Red yarn

Preparation:

Tie a piece of red yarn around the right wrist of each child.

How to play:

Chorus:
Jesus gave me a foot.
Jesus gave me a hand.
Jesus gave me an eye.
So I can do all that I can.

Verse:
I put my right hand in,
I put my right hand out,
I give my right hand a
Shake, shake, shake,
and turn myself about.

(Insert left hand, right foot, left foot, right hip, left hip, backside, head, whole self.)

1. Sing to the tune of "Looby Loo."
2. The children stand in a circle and act out the words to the song.
3. While the children are singing the chorus, they walk forward to the center of the circle and then back out.
4. The chorus is repeated after each verse.

Game 5. Hot Potato (Age 7-9)

You will need:

One potato, mystery box, Bible questions on strips of paper

How to play:

1. The children form a circle.
2. One child is "It."
3. "It" says, "Pass the potato."
4. The player who has the potato must pass it to his left.
5. "It" calls out, "Hot potato!"
6. Whoever is caught with the potato is "It."
7. "It" must pay a forfeit by answering a question from the mystery box.

Game 6. Carpet Stomp (Age 7-10)

You will need:

Record player or piano music, carpet sample (or mark off a square on the floor with chalk or tape)

How to play:

1. The children march in a circle in time to the music.
2. When a child steps on the carpet, he must name a book of the Bible or a Bible friend.
3. He must say the name quickly. If the music stops before he steps off the carpet, he is out of the game.
4. The last child standing wins the game.

Game 7. Bible Hopscotch (Age 7-12)

You will need:

Cards, chalk

Preparation:

1. Write Bible questions on cards.
2. Draw a hopscotch pattern on the floor with chalk or tape, as shown in the diagram.
3. Place one question card in every numbered box.

How to play:

1. The child stands in front of box one. He must hop into space one with one foot, pick up the question, turn with a hop, and hop out again.
2. If he answers the question correctly, he hops into space one on one foot; then he hops again with the right foot into space two and the left foot into space three. He picks up question number 2, hops to reverse feet, hops with one foot into space one, and hops out again.
3. If he answers the question correctly, he goes through the same process for space three.
4. When he tries for space four, he hops into space one with one foot, space two and three together, then hops with one foot into space four.
5. He may continue until he makes a mistake.
6. On his second turn, he continues from the last question he answered correctly.
7. As they are answered, replace the questions with new ones.
8. The first child to finish space ten is the winner.

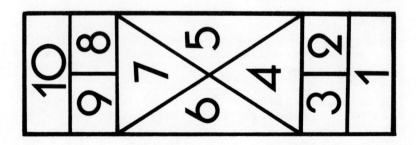

Game 8. Hidden Treasures (Age 5-7)

You will need:

A spool of thread or ball of twine for each player, picture of an eye, hand, nose, mouth, ear, foot, rainbow, bread, heart, etc.

Preparation:

1. Unwind each ball of twine or thread over, around, and under the furniture to one of the pictures before the children arrive.

How to play:

1. Give each child a ball of twine.
2. All the children start at once to wind up their twine.
3. Each child returns to the circle with his picture and tells about God's gift to us and what it does.

Game 9. I See Something Jesus Made (Age 5-7)

Preparation:

None

How to play:

1. One child is "It."
2. "It" says, "I see something Jesus made."
3. "It" describes a body part. *(Example: "It has nails.")*
4. The other children try to guess the body part from the clue.
5. If the other children can't guess, "It" gives another clue.
6. The children can guess once after each clue.
7. The child who guesses correctly becomes "It."

Game 10. Riddles (Age 5-7)

Preparation:

None

How to play:

1. The teacher calls out a riddle and the children try to guess the answer.
2. I can wink, I can cry, tell me please who am I?
3. I can sniff, I can sneeze, say my name if you please.
4. I hear sound, low and high, tell me now, who am I?
5. I can sing, talk, and pray, say my name without delay.
6. I can help you count to ten, if you guess me then you win.
7. Walk, run, jump, hop! Say my name before I pop!

Game 11. Jesus Says (Age 7-10)

Preparation:

None

How to play:

1. The teacher can lead this game. It is played like "Simon Says."
2. The children imitate the activity when the caller uses the prefix, "Jesus Says."
3. The child is out of the game if he imitates the action when the teacher leaves out "Jesus Says."

(Suggested calls: Jesus says pray, Jesus says sing, hit your neighbor, Jesus says read His Word, squint, Jesus says tiptoe, stomp.)

Game 12. Drop the Question (Age 7-12)

You will need:

Question cards, mystery box

Preparation:

1. Put questions on cards.
2. Put cards in mystery box.

How to play:

1. The children stand in a circle.
2. "It" picks a question from the mystery box in the middle of the circle.
3. "It" skips around the outside of the circle.
4. He drops the card behind a child and gives a command *(baby step, slide, skip, etc.)*
5. The child picks up the card and gives the correct answer.
6. The teacher gives the signal to go, and both carry out the command in the opposite direction around the circle.
7. The child who gets to the open space is safe, and the other child becomes "It."
8. If the question isn't answered, "It" picks another card and repeats the process with another child.

Game 13. Bible Book Hunt (Age 7-12)

You will need:

Cards

Preparation:

1. Make a set of cards. One Bible book is written on each card.
2. The Old Testament will make up one set, and the New Testament will make up a second set.

3. When playing this game with young children, do not use all of a set.

How to play:

1. Mix the cards and pass them out to the children.
2. Each child looks at his cards but keeps them hidden.
3. For the New Testament, the child who has Matthew must find Mark by asking another child, "Are you Mark?"
4. The child answers, "I am not Mark," or "Yes, I am Mark."
5. The cards are laid out in a row.
6. When Mark has been found, he must find Luke, and so forth, until all the cards are in order.

Game 14. Bible Hunt (Age 7-12)

You will need:

Bible pictures, colored paper, foam ball, chalk

Preparation:

1. Paste pictures of Bible characters on colored pieces of paper or tagboard.
2. Attach the pictures to a wall.

How to play:

1. A child throws a soft foam ball at one of the pictures.
2. If the ball hits the picture, the child tells the Bible story the picture represents.

Adaption for older children:

1. Attach numbers to the wall.
2. The child must answer the question that has the same number.
3. He would receive the same number of points as the question he answers.

Game 15. Bible Book Hop (Age 7-12)

Preparation:

1. Draw a hopscotch pattern on the floor.
2. Change the letters after each game.

How to play:

1. As the child hops, he must name a book of the Bible that begins with that letter.
2. The next child repeats the action, but he must use different books.
3. If a Bible book is repeated, the child loses his turn.

Adaption:

Use the names of Bible characters or places.

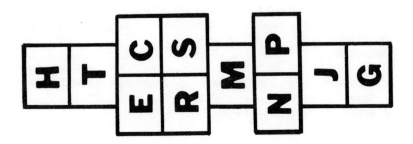

Game 16. Bible Verse Game (Age 7-10)

You will need:

Paper strips

Preparation:

1. Write Bible verses with key words left out on sentence strips.

How to play:

1. Divide into teams.
2. Each team tries in turn to guess the missing words.
3. The first team to guess correctly wins one point.

Game 17. Bible Friends (Age 9-12)

You will need:

Pencil and paper for each child

How to play:

1. Give each child a piece of paper and a pencil.
2. Each child lists as many Bible friends as he can in ten minutes.
3. The child with the longest list wins.

Game 18. Bible Baseball (Age 7-12)

You will need:

Cardboard cards with Bible questions, mystery box

Preparation:

1. Make signs that read first, second, third, home, pitcher.
2. Place the signs around the room in the shape of a baseball diamond.
3. Prepare a set of Bible questions.

How to play:

1. Divide into teams.
2. The pitcher takes a card from the stack or mystery box and reads the question to the batter.
3. If the batter gives the correct answer, he hops to first base.
4. If the next batter answers the question, he hops to first base and the player there hops to second base.
5. Difficult questions have the word "home run" written on the card.
6. If a player misses a question, his team is out and the other team is up to bat.
7. The team who answers the most questions wins.

Game 19. Bust a Question (Age 7-12)

You will need:

Paper, balloons, bulletin board, darts

Preparation:

1. Write Bible questions on thin strips of paper.
2. Roll into tiny balls and slip inside balloons.
3. Blow up the balloons and tie them.
4. Attach the balloons to the bulletin board.

How to play:

1. The children stand behind a designated line.
2. A child throws a dart at the balloons. If he breaks one, he gets one point.
3. If he can answer the Bible question, he receives two points.
4. The child or team with the most points wins the game.

Game 20. Bible Stairs (Age 7-10)

You will need:

Cards, chalk

Preparation:

1. Make a set of cards with Bible questions written on them.
2. Use tape or chalk to make a stair pattern on the floor.

How to play:

1. Divide into teams.
2. The first child on one team hops up the stairs on his right foot.
3. He stands on the top and is asked a Bible question taken from the cards.
4. After answering the question, he hops down the stairs on his left foot.

Adaption:

Use a choir stand or boxes and build a pyramid for the children to hop up and down.

Game 21. Bible Train (Age 5-10)

Preparation:

None

How to play:

1. One child (engine) moves around the room using his left arm in a circular motion to show a train moving. He "toots" like a train whistle.
2. The "train" stops at a child's chair and calls out, "All aboard the Bible Train!"
3. That child must answer by telling something he did that pleases Jesus.
4. He then attaches himself to the engine by placing his right hand on the right shoulder of the engine.
5. The game continues with the last child being the conductor each time.

Game 22. Throw-a-Question (Age 7-12)

You will need:

Large cardboard box, beanbag

Preparation:

1. Make a target board from a large cardboard box.
2. Cut as shown on the diagram.
3. Turn the box over. Cut holes in the box. Number the holes.
4. You can paint silly faces or flowers around the holes.

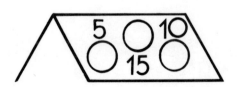 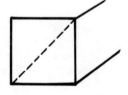

How to play:

1. The children stand three to five feet away.
2. They throw the beanbag at one of the holes.
3. If the bag goes into a hole marked 5, they must answer a question from stack number 5.
4. Points for their score are the same as the number of the question.

Game 23. Bible Balance Quiz (Age 7-12)

You will need:

Cards, mystery box

Preparation:

1. Prepare Bible questions on the cards.

How to play:

1. Designate a starting line and a finish line.
2. Divide the class into teams.
3. One child chooses a question from the mystery box and places it into his Bible.
4. The child places the Bible on top of his head.
5. The teacher says "Go!"
6. The child tries to get to the finish line without dropping his Bible.
7. At the finish line he must answer the Bible question.

Adaption:

1. Place several unbreakable objects on a tray.
2. The first child from each team starts out holding his tray at about ear level.
3. The teacher says, "Go!" and gives a command such as hop, run, slide, rabbit jump, elephant walk, etc.
4. The children follow the command as they try to reach the finish line.
5. At the finish line they must answer the Bible question.

6. They get one point for every item left on the tray, and they get two points for answering the question correctly.

Game 24. Mystery Box Game (Age 4-12)

You will need:

1. An old globe or box with a lid
2. Paint or adhesive paper
3. Bright-colored Bible pictures

Preparation:

1. Cut a hole in the top of the globe or box.
2. Paint a bright color or cover with adhesive paper.
3. Glue or paint pictures on the outside.

Mystery Objects:

1. Use model shapes of stars, artificial fruit, toy animals, vegetables.

How to play:

1. Tell a child to reach into the mystery box and pull out one item.
2. Teacher: "What did Jesus make?"
3. Child: "Jesus made _____."
4. The child should try to name the object without looking at it.
5. Use this same mystery box to hold questions for many of the games listed in this book.

Game 25. Night and Day (Age 5-7)

You will need:

Posterboard for one moon sign, one sun sign, one earth sign, flashlight, globe or large ball

Preparation:

1. Make signs.

How to play:

1. One child stands with the flashlight. Put the sun sign around his neck.
2. One child holds the globe and wears the moon sign.
3. You explain: "The earth, stars, and moon were made by God. They were made to give us night and day. The earth is turning slowly all the time."
4. Have the child with the earth sign turn slowly.
5. Say: "As the part we live on turns toward the sun, we have day."
6. Have the child hold the flashlight on the earth.
7. The earth child turns until he faces the moon.
8. Let the children take turns. Have them face the sun and say "Day" and say "Night" when they face the moon.

Game 26. Fishing (Age 5-12)

You will need:

Broomstick or tree limb, string, magnet, construction paper or tag-board, paper clip, bucket or pan

Preparation:

1. Tie a string to the end of a tree limb or a broomstick to make a fishing pole. Tie a magnet to the end of the string.
2. Trace 12 fish on construction paper or tagboard.
3. Attach a paper clip to each fish.
4. Paint the numbers 1 through 12 on the fish.

How to play:

1. Place the fish in a bucket or pan.
2. Let each child take turns catching a fish.
3. If a child catches fish number 1, he would receive a card with the first word of a Scripture verse on it.
4. After all the fish are caught (use as many of the twelve as needed), line the children up with their cards in numerical order. Read the verse to them.

    1 2   3   4   5   6   7   8 9   10
In the beginning God created the heaven and the earth. (Genesis 1:1)

Adaption:

For older children you can attach questions to the fish.

Game 27. Fins, Feathers, and Fur (Age 5-7)

Preparation:

None

How to play:

1. One person is the leader.
2. The children stand with their hands to their sides.
3. The leader says, "God made the goldfish."
4. The children should recognize that a goldfish has fins and lives in the water, so they are to put their hands behind their back.
5. If the leader says, "God made the bluebird," the children are to put their hands over their heads because the leader has named an animal with feathers.
6. If it is a furry animal, they put their hands to their shoulders.
7. If a player misses the signal he is out of the game.

Fins	Fur	Feathers
goldfish	squirrel	bluebird
catfish	dog	cardinal
dolphin	cat	wren
perch	mouse	sparrow
sunfish	lion	parrot
rainbow trout	bear	parakeet
guppy	tiger	bluebird
salmon	leopard	mockingbird
puffer fish	panther	swan
angler fish	rabbit	duck
speckled trout	raccoon	turkey
angelfish	polar bear	chicken

Game 28. Did You Ever See? (Age 5-7)

You will need:

Animal pictures, mystery box

Preparation:

1. Place pictures of animals in the mystery box.
2. Animals must have two syllables such as redfish, puppy, lion, giraffe, donkey, milk cow, brown horse.

How to play:

1. Sing to the tune of "Did You Ever See a Lassie?"
2. The children stand in a circle and hold hands while walking around.
3. One child stands in the center of the circle.
4. The child in the center reaches into the box and pulls out a picture of an animal.
5. He shows it to the other children.
6. The children walk in a circle and sing. The person in the center acts like a "kitty" or whatever animal is on the card.
7. During the second verse, all the children act like a "kitty."

8. The child in the center chooses the child who was the best actor to take his place.

Verse One:

Did you ever see a kitty that God made, that God made?
Did you ever see a kitty that God made for us?

Verse Two:

Do this way and that way and this way and that way,
Did you ever see a kitty that God made for us?

Game 29. Concentration (Age 6-12)

You will need:

Posterboard, pairs of Bible pictures, construction paper, glue

Preparation:

1. Put three rows of four pockets on a standard-sized piece of posterboard.
2. Use six pairs of identical pictures.
3. Mount the pictures on construction paper. The paper must be sized to fit into the pockets.

How to play:

1. Put the pictures facedown in the pockets.
2. The first child may turn over two pictures. If they match, he scores one point.
3. If they don't match, the cards are turned facedown once more.
4. The next child tries to remember the position of the cards and turn over a match.
5. The child with the most matches wins the game.

Game 30. Clothespin Friend Relay (Age 6-10)

You will need:

Snap-type clothespins, cardboard

Preparation:

1. Get snap-type clothespins.
2. Write the names of Bible characters on squares of cardboard.

How to play:

1. Divide into two teams.
2. Each team stands or sits in a line.
3. Each child has a clothespin.
4. The children pass the card with their clothespin.
5. As the child passes the card, he must tell a fact he has learned about that character before he passes it on.
6. The team that passes the card first to the end of the line wins.

Game 31. Ask and Pitch (Age 7-12)

You will need:

A large rubber ball

Preparation:

None

How to play:

1. The children stand in a circle.
2. Assign a different number to each child.

3. "It" stands in the middle of the circle and throws the ball up in the air. As he throws, "It" calls out one of the numbers.
4. The number that is called runs to catch the ball on the first bounce.
5. The child who catches the ball must name a Bible book, tell something that pleases God, or answer a Bible question.
6. If he does this, he throws the ball and calls a number.
7. If he cannot do this, he loses his turn.

Game 32. I Can Please God (Age 5-9)

Preparation:

None

How to play:

1. Form a circle.
2. One child stands in the center and calls on all the children who have on yellow clothing.
3. Each one comes to the center and does a certain task as required by "It," such as hop on one foot, walk like a duck, etc.
4. Each then tells something he can do to please God.
5. "It" then chooses someone to take his place.

Game 33. David and Goliath (Age 6-10)

Preparation:

None

How to play:

1. One child is chosen to be David and one is chosen to be Goliath.

2. The other children join hands and form a circle. David is in the center and Goliath is on the outside.
3. The players in the circle do everything they can to keep Goliath from catching David.
4. If Goliath does get into the circle, they let David out and try to keep Goliath inside.
5. They must keep their hands joined at all times.
6. If Goliath catches David, the two join the circle and others take their places.

Game 34. Help Me! (Age 6-10)

Preparation:

None

How to play:

1. The children stand in a circle.
2. One child is David and stands in the center.
3. David says, "Help me find my sheep," to one of the children.
4. David describes several things about the clothing of one of the children until the child being described recognizes himself.
5. The sheep begins to run around the circle with David after him.
6. If David catches him, the sheep becomes the next David.

Game 35. Bowling to Please God (Age 6-10)

You will need:

Paper, carton, ball, mystery box

Preparation:

1. Get a small cardboard carton and a ball.
2. Write messages on slips of paper that are pleasing to God and messages that are not pleasing to God. Put in your mystery box.

How to play:

1. Divide into teams.
2. The children take turns rolling the balls into the carton.
3. Each time the ball enters the carton, that child may take a slip of paper and read the message.
4. If the message is pleasing to God, that team gets a point.
5. The team with the most points wins the game.

Messages that please God:

1. Share my toys.
2. Help mother wash dishes.
3. Tell the truth when I break something.
4. Sit quietly in worship service.
5. Pray for a sick friend.
6. Say please and thank you.
7. Walk when I'm in God's house.
8. Sing songs about Jesus.
9. Tell a friend that Jesus loves him.
10. Read my Bible every day.
11. Study for a test at school.

Messages that do not please God:

1. Hit my brother when he plays with my toys.
2. Go outside and play while my mother washes the dishes.
3. Blame my dog for breaking something that I broke.
4. Wiggle and whisper during worship service.
5. Turn the TV up loud when my daddy has a headache.
6. Forget to say please and thank you.
7. Run and talk loud in God's house.
8. Tell a friend that I don't like someone because they look ugly.
9. Scatter my toys all over the house.
10. Use bad words when I'm angry.
11. Look at someone's paper during a test at school.

Game 36. Feeling for Bible Questions (Age 6-12)

You will need:

Cards, sandpaper, scissors, glue, mystery box

Preparation:

1. Paste sandpaper numbers on 4 x 6 index cards. Give each card a points number.
2. Make a list of Bible questions.

How to play:

1. Place the cards in the mystery box.
2. Divide the class into two teams.
3. The first child of each team hops to the mystery box across the room.
4. He picks out a card without peeking and tries to figure out the number by feeling.
5. If he knows the number, he is given a Bible question that corresponds to your prepared question list.
6. Number 1 card would receive question number 1.
7. If he correctly answers the question, his team receives the number of points on the card.
8. He hops back to the line and another takes a turn.

Game 37. Find My Sheep (Age 5-7)

Preparation:

None

How to play:

1. The teacher plays the part of Jesus.

2. Read Matthew 28:19. Choose a child to be a missionary who will carry out the instructions in this verse.
3. The teacher says to the child, "Please find my sheep. My sheep is wearing _____." (She describes the clothing of one of the children in the room.)
4. The missionary child walks around the room looking for the child who was described.
5. He takes the child to Jesus and that child becomes the missionary.

Game 38. Getting Acquainted (Age 6-10)

Preparation:

None

How to play:

1. One child is "It."
2. He hides his eyes.
3. Another child leaves the room.
4. All the children change places.
5. "It" turns around and tries to guess who is missing before the others slowly count to ten.
6. Repeat until all have a turn.

Game 39 Guess Who? (Age 6-10)

You will need:

Newspapers, butcher paper, sheet

Preparation:

1. Tape newspapers or butcher paper between two chairs or hang

an old sheet across a cord. Cut two eyeholes at a height where the children can sit in a chair and look through.

How to play:

1. Let one person at a time sit in front while the other children take turns looking through the holes.
2. The person who is "It" must identify those peeking through the holes by saying, "Jesus loves _____."

Game 40. Hopscotch Bible Facts (Age 6-10)

You will need:

Chalk, tape

Preparation:

1. Mark a letter pattern of your choice on the floor with chalk or masking tape.
2. Label each row Place, Person, Book.

Place	Person	Book
B	P	M
S	J	A
C	T	J

How to play:

1. Divide into teams.
2. The child jumps from left to right and names a Bible person, Bible place, or Bible book that begins with the letter in the square.
3. He may continue for three jumps as long as he can name a person, place, or book of the Bible.
4. He must jump from left to right, even into the first square of the row he chooses.
5. His team receives one point for each correct answer.

Game 41. Headache Questions (Age 6-12)

You will need:

Cards

Preparation:

1. Make out question cards.
2. Put questions under chair of King or Queen.

How to play:

1. One child in the circle is King or Queen.
2. Each player tries to reach the King (Queen) and get a card with a Bible question from under the chair.
3. If the player can answer the question, he becomes the King or Queen.
4. If he hears the player, the King (Queen) groans and holds his head. The noise is so loud his head hurts.
5. The player must then go back to the circle.

Game 42. I Saw Something God Made (Age 5-7)

Preparation:

None

How to play:

1. A circle is formed with one "It" in the middle.
2. "It" says, "On my way to church this morning, I saw something God made. I saw _____."
3. He then imitates what he saw.
4. The others guess what he saw.
5. If no one guesses, the one in the center must tell what he saw and choose someone to take his place.
6. It cannot be a man-made article.

Game 43. Jacob's Ladder (Age 7-10)

You will need:

Cards, chalk, tape, spinner

Preparation:

1. Write the names of Bible characters on cards.
2. Draw a ladder on the floor with chalk or tape. Place a card under each rung.

How to play:

1. Divide the class into two teams.
2. Spin a spinner to see how many steps can be hopped.
3. The player must hop the number of steps indicated.
4. He must tell a Bible fact about the name he lands on.
5. If the next child lands on the same name, he must tell a different Bible fact.
6. Each child receives one point for each answer.
7. The team with the most points wins the game.

Game 44. Kick a Bible Question (Age 7-10)

You will need:

Large rubber ball, cards

Preparation:

1. Get a large rubber ball.
2. Make three large number cards (1-3).
3. Make three sets of numbers, one for each of the cards.

How to play:

1. A child stands a short distance away from the cards.
2. He kicks the ball at a number.
3. The teacher gives him a Bible question from that set which corresponds with the number card he hits with the ball.
4. If he can answer the question, he receives that number of points.

Game 45. Smile, Jesus Loves You (Age 5-10)

Preparation:

None

How to play:

1. The children stand in a circle.
2. "It" stands in the middle and moves from child to child.
3. He points to one and says, "Smile, Jesus loves you."
4. The one to whom he is pointing must say, "The same to you," before "It" is finished.
5. If "It" points and doesn't say anything, the child mustn't say anything either.
6. The child who makes a mistake, becomes "It."

Game 46. This Is the Way (Age 5-8)

Preparation:

None

How to play:

1. Sing to the tune of "Mulberry Bush."
2. The children walk in a circle and sing.
3. The children imitate the action indicated in the verse.

Verses:

(Walk in a circle.)

This is the way we go to church, go to church, go to church.
This is the way we go to church, on a Sunday morning.

(Pretend to hold a Bible and read.)

This is the way we read our Bible, read our Bible, read our Bible.
This is the way we read our Bible, so early in the morning.

(Pretend to pray.)

This is the way we say our prayers, say our prayers, say our prayers.
This is the way we say our prayers, so early in the morning.

(Pretend to tiptoe.)

This is the way we walk in church, walk in church, walk in church.
This is the way we walk in church, so early in the morning.

(Shake hands with one another.)

This is the way we say hello, say hello, say hello.
This is the way we say hello, on a Sunday morning.

(Pretend to pass the collection plate.)

This is the way we give to God, give to God, give to God.
This is the way we give to God, on a Sunday morning.

(Bow head.)

This is the way we bow our head, bow our head, bow our head.
This is the way we bow our head, so early in the morning.

(Walk in a circle.)

This is the way we go home from church, go home from church, go home
  from church.
This is the way we go home from church, on a Sunday morning.

Game 47. Jesus' World (Age 7-12)

You will need:

A clock with a second hand, Bible map

How to play:

1. Choose two teams.
2. One person or team picks out a name on a Bible map.
3. The other team or player has thirty seconds to find this spot.
4. If he does, he earns a point for his team.
5. The game is over when one team has earned five points.

36

Game 48. Crossing the Red Sea (Age 6-9)

You will need:

Chalk

Preparation:

1. Draw two parallel lines on the floor to represent the Red Sea.

How to play:

1. Each child steps across the lines without touching them.
2. The lines are then widened. Again the children must step across.
3. They continue until they fall or step into the Red Sea.
4. They must step across. They can't jump across.
5. The last one left in the game is the winner.

Game 49. Bible Picture Slide (Age 5-10)

You will need:

Pictures

Preparation:

1. Prepare a set of modern or Bible pictures.
2. Hang a rope across the room or chalkboard.
3. Place a curtain ring, ring clip, or tie a loop to a clothespin and attach to the rope.
4. Attach one picture to each ring, clip, or loop.

How to play:

1. The first child must skip to the rope and take the ring, clip, or loop in his hand.

2. He slides it from left to right to the end of the rope.
3. He takes the picture from its holder and tells the story in the picture.

Adaption:

Use questions on the holders for older children.

Game 50. Memory Game (Age 7-12)

You will need:

Bible pictures

Preparation:

1. Find 15 Bible pictures. Each picture must tell a different Bible story.

How to play:

1. Place all the Bible pictures on the table.
2. Cover the pictures with a cloth.
3. When the cloth is removed, allow the children two minutes to look at the pictures.
4. They then have five minutes to list as many Bible stories as they can remember from the pictures that they have just seen.
5. The child with the longest list wins.

Game 51. Noah's Ark (Age 5-7)

You will need:

Three-foot piece of butcher paper, two chairs, masking tape

Preparation:

1. Fasten the paper with tape to the two chairs for an ark.

How to play:

1. Play and sing to the tune of "The Farmer in the Dell."
2. The children stand in front of the paper ark.
3. One child is chosen to be Noah. He stands behind the ark.
4. The children sing the song. They pause at the end of, "Noah takes a _____," long enough to choose an animal.
5. Noah comes from behind the ark and chooses a child to be a dog, cat, horse, cow, etc.
6. The child who is chosen joins Noah behind the ark.
7. After all the children have been chosen, they sing the last verse of the song.

Song:

Noah's in his ark. Noah's in his ark. Listen to the thunder roll. Noah's in his ark.

Noah takes a _____. Noah takes a _____. Listen to the thunder roll. Noah takes a _____.

God shut the door. God shut the door. Listen to the thunder roll. God shut the door.

Game 52. Bible Quiz Run (Age 10-12)

You will need:

Cards, beanbags

Preparation:

1. Prepare Bible verses on cards with one word left out.
2. Paste a picture on the other side.
3. Draw a starting line and a finishing line.

How to play:

1. Divide into teams.
2. Two children with beanbags stand at the starting line.
3. They throw the beanbags at the card and try to move the card toward the goal line.
4. Each child in the teams throws once until the card reaches the finish line.
5. The player who threw the last beanbag picks up the card and brings it back to the team.
6. The team tries to figure out the missing word.
7. The captain races to the chalkboard and writes the word under their team name.
8. The race begins again with another card.
9. The team with the most words on the board wins the game.
10. Read aloud the finished Bible verses.

Game 53. Paul (Age 9-12)

You will need:

Heavy paper, two jars, dried beans

Preparation:

1. Make a paper box. See pattern.
2. Push a pencil through so it will spin like a top.
3. Print "P" on one side of the box; "A" on the second side; "U" on the third side; and "L" on the fourth side.
4. Make up a set of questions about Paul. The questions should be divided into one, two, three, or four points per question.

How to play:

1. Divide into teams.
2. Spin the top.
3. If the "P" turns up, ask a four-point question. If "A" shows up, ask a three-point question. If "U" turns up, ask a two-point question. And "L" is worth one point.
4. Use two jars. Each team will get four beans for a four-point question to put in their jar, three for a three-point question, etc.
5. The team with the most beans wins the game.

Note: The beans in the jar are a good way for younger children and learning-impaired students to keep track of their scores in any game.

Game 54. Fishers of Men (Age 6-9)

Preparation:

None

How to play:

1. One child pretends to be Peter.
2. Peter says, "Who would like to be fishers of men?"
3. All the children get in line and march behind him, pretending to row a boat with their arms.
4. When Peter calls out, "Jesus loves you," all of the children race back to their chairs.
5. The first one back to his seat is Peter for the next fishing trip.

Game 55. Bible Picture Charades (Age 6-12)

You will need:

Bible pictures

Preparation:

1. Cut out Bible pictures that show Bible characters in action.

How to play:

1. Put the pictures facedown on the table.
2. A child comes to the table, picks out a picture, and imitates the action.
3. The child then tells in his own words what he thinks is happening in the picture.

Game 56. Put Together Quiz (Age 10-12)

You will need:

Strips of paper, pictures, cardboard, paste or glue

Preparation:

1. Prepare Bible questions on strips of paper from the Bible unit you are studying.
2. Paste two pictures on cardboard. These can be pictures of flowers, birds, cars, etc.
3. Cut the pictures into pieces.

How to play:

1. Divide into teams.
2. The first team draws a question.
3. If the first child answers the question correctly, he may pick out a part of the puzzle to be assembled and place it on the flannelboard or table.
4. The second team then draws a question.
5. The team that finishes their puzzle first wins the game.

Game 57. Be a Super Star (Age 6-12)

You will need:

Rope, box, chair, books, cards

Preparation:

1. Arrange a maze on the floor.
2. Tape a piece of rope to the floor to walk like a tightrope.
3. Place a box, with both ends cut out, for the children to crawl through.

43

4. Place a chair to go around.
5. Place a stack of books to jump over.
6. Put Bible questions on cards and place one at each obstacle.

How to play:

1. The child walks in stocking feet on the rope, picks up the card, and answers the question.
2. He walks around the chair, picks up the question, and answers it.
3. Next, he jumps over the stack of books and answers that question. Then he crawls through the box and answers that question.
4. If the child completes the maze, he is a "Super Star."
5. Change the questions for the next child.

Game 58. Ring a Happy Face (Age 6-9)

You will need:

Egg carton, suckers, paper, jar rings

Preparation:

1. Turn an egg carton upside down. Stick suckers in each cup.
2. Paste smiley faces on six suckers and sad faces on six suckers.
3. Find six jar rings, or other round objects, to throw over the suckers.

How to play:

1. The children throw the jar rings at the suckers.
2. If they ring a happy face, they must tell something they could do that pleases God.
3. They can keep the suckers they ring.
4. Provide for the child who doesn't ring a sucker by asking him to tell something he has done that week that pleased God.

Game 59. Secret Message Game (Age 6-10)

You will need:

Paper, candy, small box, wrapping paper

Preparation:

1. Write a secret message on a piece of paper. The message could be a Scripture verse or something like, "Smile, Jesus loves you."
2. Put the message and a piece of candy in a small box. Wrap the box with as many layers of paper as you have time and inclination.
3. Be sure there are as many layers as there are children.
4. Use very little tape, so the wrappings will come off easily.

How to play:

1. Seat the children in a circle.
2. Pass the box around.
3. Each child removes one layer of paper.
4. The child who takes off the last layer of paper finds a message and a surprise.

Game 60. Scripture Chain (Age 7-10)

You will need:

Construction paper

Preparation:

1. Cut construction paper into 1 x 6 inch strips.
2. Write one word of the day's Bible verse on each piece of paper.
3. Give each child a complete Scripture.
4. Paste or glue strips together.

How to play:

1. Show the children how to make a paper chain.
2. Children begin at once to put their chain together.
3. The chain must spell out the Bible verse of the day.
4. The first child to finish is the winner.

Game 61. Lollipop Scriptures (Age 7-10)

You will need:

Suckers

Preparation:

1. Write one word from the week's memory Scripture on a sucker until the Scripture is completed.
2. Line the suckers up at random at the end of the room for a finish line.
3. Keep the sucker that has the Scripture reference on it.
4. Be sure to have one more player than you have suckers.

How to play:

1. When the signal is given, the children should race to the finish line and grab a sucker.
2. The child who doesn't receive a sucker is given one and told to sit down. He is eliminated.
3. The children should then try to work out the Scripture message. They can stand in a row so the message is in order.
4. Each child keeps his sucker.

Game 62. Step by Step With Jesus (Age 6-10)

You will need:

Cards, chalk

Preparation:

1. Prepare a set of direction cards with words like these on them: One giant step, two baby steps, three scissors steps, two slides, one hop, one skip, etc.
2. Write Bible questions on another set of cards.
3. Draw a line on the floor.

How to play:

1. The children stand way behind the line on the floor.
2. The teacher takes a card from each set and reads the question.
3. If the child answers correctly, he may take the number of steps indicated on the card.
4. The first child who reaches the finish line wins the game.

Game 63. Scripture Match Up (Age 6-10)

You will need:

Plastic eggs, egg cartons, tape, paper

Preparation:

1. Tape half of a Scripture to each part of a plastic egg.
2. Hide the halves in separate places.

How to play:

1. The children try to find the matching Scriptures.
2. Count the eggs and give one point for each complete Scripture.
3. Read the Scripture to the group.
4. Use egg cartons to hold the eggs.

Game 64. Bible Truth in Action (Age 6-12)

You will need:

Cards

Preparation:

1. Prepare a set of simple sentences or pictures that illustrate one of the Ten Commandments, a Bible truth, or Bible story.

How to play:

1. One child chooses a card and acts out the sentence or picture.
2. The other children try to guess what is on the card from the acting.
3. The child who guesses correctly gets the next turn.

Game 65. Scripture Skip (Age 7-10)

You will need:

Sheet music, cards

Preparation:

1. Choose a piece of music to which children can skip.

2. Prepare a set of Scriptures.
3. Cut the Scriptures in half.

How to play:

1. Give each child half of a Scripture.
2. The children skip while the music plays.
3. When the music stops, the children try to find the other half of their Scripture before the music begins again.
4. The music is played again, and the children who have not found their second half begin to skip.
5. The game continues until all the Scriptures are matched.
6. Read the completed Scriptures to the entire group.

Game 66. Scrambled Feelings (Age 6-10)

You will need:

Carpet squares

Preparation:

1. Use six to twelve carpet squares, depending on the number of children you have.
2. The caller doesn't have a square.
3. Assign a good feeling to all the children (love, help, kind, share, obey, truth, cooperate, pray, listen, care).

How to play:

1. The caller calls out two feelings and a direction (care and share, hop).
2. These two children try to change places before the caller gets one of their places.
3. The child who doesn't get a place is the caller.
4. When the caller says, "Jesus loves you," all the children change places.

Game 67. Scripture Hookup (Age 7-10)

You will need:

Cards, string

Preparation:

1. Make a set of cards with a Scripture verse on them. One word should be on each card.
2. Punch a hole in each card. Attach a string so it can be hung around a child's neck.
3. Pass the cards out one by one to the children.

How to play:

1. The child who has the word beginning with a capital letter walks around the room.
2. He tries to find the second word of the Scripture. When he does he hooks up with him by joining elbows.
3. The two walk around and try to find the third word.
4. Continue until all the words are in order.

Game 68. Give the Answer (Age 7-10)

You will need:

Cards, mystery box

Preparation:

1. Prepare Bible questions and place in the mystery box.

How to play:

1. The children form a circle.
2. One person is chosen to be "It."
3. The children in the circle close their eyes and cup their hands behind their back.
4. "It" gets a question from the mystery box and runs around the circle.
5. He drops the question into a child's hand.
6. The question is read and answered by that child.
7. Then "It" and this child stand back to back. When the teacher says "Go," they begin to run.
8. They race around the circle to the empty space.
9. The one without a space is "It."

Game 69. Bag a Book (Age 7-10)

You will need:

Cards, bucket, beanbags, or tennis balls

Preparation:

1. Make cards with the names of the books of the Bible on them.
2. Place a bucket on the floor, about four feet from the children.
3. Get some beanbags or tennis balls.

How to play:

1. Divide into teams.
2. The first child throws a ball or beanbag at the bucket.
3. If it lands in the bucket, the child must pick a card from the bucket and tell whether the Bible book is in the Old or New Testament.
4. If he cannot name where it is found, he must return the card to the bucket.
5. If he names it correctly, his team keeps the card.
6. The team with the most cards wins the game.

Game 70. Truth Target (Age 7-10)

You will need:

Target, beanbag, cards

Preparation:

1. Place a large target on the floor.
2. Use different colors for degrees of difficulty.
3. Get a beanbag.
4. Prepare questions of four degrees of difficulty.

How to play:

1. The child throws the beanbag.
2. If it lands on the outside ring, which might be yellow, he would have to answer a yellow question worth one point.
3. If the beanbag landed on the second circle, he would receive a question worth two points.
4. If the beanbag landed on the third circle, he would receive a question worth three points.
5. If it landed on the bull's-eye, he would receive a question worth four points.

Game 71. Feelings Bounce (Age 6-10)

You will need:

Shoe boxes, paper, rubber ball

Preparation:

1. Staple three shoe boxes together.
2. Glue or draw a happy face, a mad face, and a sad face on each of the boxes.

How to play:

1. The child bounces a rubber ball on the floor, aimed at one of the boxes.
2. If the ball lands in the happy box, the child must tell something that makes him happy. If it lands in the sad box, he must tell something that makes him sad. If it lands in the mad box, he must tell something that makes him mad.

Game 72. Hook a Question (Age 7-12)

You will need:

Hooks, cardboard, jar rings

Preparation:
1. Place 25 cup hooks on the face of a piece of cardboard.
2. Prepare one-point, two-point, three-point, four-point, and five-point questions. The bonus questions are 10 points.

How to play:
1. The children stand six feet from the board.
2. They throw jar rings at the cup hooks.
3. When they ring a cup hook, they must answer a question from that numbered stack. The winner is the one with the most points.

Game 73. Witness Chain (Age 6-10)

Preparation:
None

How to play:
1. One child is a missionary.
2. He runs and tries to tag another child.
3. When he touches the child, he says, "Jesus loves you."
4. That child must join hands with the missionary and he tags another child.
5. Both say, "Jesus loves you," when the tag is made.
6. The third child joins the group.
7. Only the last child can tag.
8. The tag doesn't count if the chain is broken.

Game 74. Witness for Jesus (Age 5-7)

Preparation:
None

How to play:
1. Two children hold their hands up to form a bridge.
2. All the other children walk under the bridge.
3. The teacher says, "Witness!"
4. The children lower their hands and say, "Jesus loves _____."
5. The game continues until all the children are caught.

Game 75. Who "Dun" It? (Age 7-10)

You will need:
Shoe boxes, cards

Preparation:
1. Staple together six shoe boxes, three on top of three.
2. Label each section with the name of a Bible person.
3. Make fact cards about the characters you choose.

How to play:
1. Each team has an equal number of cards.
2. Each child takes his turn. He must hop, skip, and jump to the box.
3. He places his card in the section that matches his Bible fact.
4. Then he moves to the end of the line.
5. The team wins that gets the most facts in the boxes correctly.

Adaption:
Pictures can be used for younger or learning-impaired students.

Game 76. Teaspoon Questions (Age 7-12)

You will need:
String, paper, teaspoons

Preparation:
1. Tape a piece of string to the floor.
2. Write Bible questions on paper and wad them up small enough to fit on a teaspoon.

How to play:
1. Divide into teams and line up.
2. Give the first person on each team a teaspoon with a Bible question on it.
3. The child must put the handle of the teaspoon in his mouth and walk the string without dropping the question.
4. At the end of the line, he unwads the question, reads it, and answers it.
5. The next person must follow.
6. The team that answers the most questions correctly wins the game.

BIBLE QUESTIONS

About the Bible:

1. Who made the heavens and the earth? (Genesis 1:1)
2. How long did it take God to make the world and everything in it? (Genesis 1:31)
3. What did God think about everything He had made? (Genesis 1:31)
4. What did God do on the seventh day? (Genesis 2:2)
5. What was the name of the special home God made for the first man? (Genesis 2:8)
6. What was the name of the first man? (Genesis 2:19)
7. What was the name of the first woman? (Genesis 4:1)
8. What shape did the devil use when he talked to Eve? (Genesis 3:1)
9. What did God tell Adam and Eve not to do? (Genesis 3:3)
10. Why were the man and the woman afraid to meet God after they had eaten the fruit? (Genesis 3:10)
11. Who was the first child born to Adam and Eve? (Genesis 4:1)
12. Who was the second child? (Genesis 4:2)
13. What kind of work did Abel do? (Genesis 4:2)
14. What kind of work did Cain do? (Genesis 4:2)
15. What kind of offering did Cain bring to the Lord? (Genesis 4:3)
16. What kind of offering did Abel bring to the Lord? (Genesis 4:4)
17. Whose offering did the Lord accept? (Genesis 4:4)
18. Which brother became a murderer? (Genesis 4:8)
19. What did Cain say when God asked him about his brother? (Genesis 4:9)
20. What was the name of the man who did not die? (Genesis 5:24)
21. What was the name of the man who lived longer than anyone else? (Genesis 5:27)
22. What did God tell Noah He was going to do? (Genesis 6:13)
23. Why was God going to destroy all the people on the earth? (Genesis 6:5)
24. What did God tell Noah to do? (Genesis 6:14)
25. How was God going to destroy the earth? (Genesis 6:17)
26. What was Noah supposed to take into the ark with him? (Genesis 6:18, 19)
27. How long did it rain on the earth? (Genesis 7:12)
28. How deep did the water get? (Genesis 7:20)
29. What was the first thing Noah did when he and his family came out of the ark? (Genesis 8:20)
30. What promise did God make to Noah after the flood? (Genesis 9:15)
31. What sign did God give to Noah after the flood? (Genesis 9:13)
32. What did God tell Abram to do? (Genesis 12:1)
33. What did God promise to Abram? (Genesis 12:2)
34. Who went with Abram? (Genesis 12:5)
35. What was the name of Abram's wife? (Genesis 12:5)
36. Who was Lot? (Genesis 12:5)
37. Why did the servants of Abram and Lot fuss? (Genesis 13:6, 7)
38. How did Abram settle the argument? (Genesis 13:9)
39. Where did Abram go? (Genesis 13:12)

40. Where did Lot go? (Genesis 13:12)
41. What kind of people lived in Sodom? (Genesis 13:13)
42. What happened to Lot while he was living in Sodom? (Genesis 14:10-12)
43. What did Abram do when he heard about this? (Genesis 14:14)
44. What did God promise to Abram because he stayed faithful and obedient? (Genesis 17:19)
45. What was the name of the son that was promised to Abram? (Genesis 17:19)
46. What new name did God give to Abram? (Genesis 17:5)
47. What did God ask Abraham to do with Isaac? (Genesis 22:2)
48. Why did God ask Abraham to do this? (Genesis 22:1)
49. What did Isaac ask Abraham about the sacrifice? (Genesis 22:7)
50. What did Abraham reply to Isaac? (Genesis 22:8)
51. Who carried the wood for the sacrifice? (Genesis 22:6)
52. What did God send to take the place of Isaac? (Genesis 22:13)
53. Where did Abraham send his servant to find a wife for Isaac? (Genesis 24:10)
54. What was the name of the girl the servant found? (Genesis 24:15)
55. How did God answer the servant's prayer to send the right girl to the well? (Genesis 24:14, 19)
56. What was the name of Rebecca's brother? (Genesis 24:29)
57. What were the names of Isaac and Rebecca's children? (Genesis 25:26)
58. What were the differences between Jacob and Esau? (Genesis 25:27)
59. What did Esau do that showed he did not care anything about his birthright? (Genesis 25:33)
60. Why did Rebecca want Jacob to have the blessing? (Genesis 25:28)
61. Why couldn't Isaac see Esau? (Genesis 27:1)
62. What did Isaac ask Esau to do? (Genesis 27:4)
63. What did Rebecca ask Jacob to do when she overheard Isaac talking to Esau? (Genesis 27:9, 10)
64. How did Jacob fool his father into thinking he was Esau? (Genesis 27:15, 16)
65. How did Esau feel when he learned Jacob had tricked Isaac into giving the blessing to him? (Genesis 27:41)
66. What did Jacob do to avoid Esau's anger? (Genesis 27:43)
67. What promise did God make to Jacob? (Genesis 28:14, 15)
68. Whom did Jacob stay with in Haran? (Genesis 29:14)
69. What did Jacob want in return for working for Laban? (Genesis 28:18)
70. How did Laban cheat Jacob? (Genesis 29:25)
71. Who went with Jacob when he decided to return to his homeland? (Genesis 31:17)
72. Why was Jacob afraid to go back? (Genesis 32:11)
73. How did Esau act when he saw Jacob? (Genesis 33:4)
74. What new name did God give to Jacob? (Genesis 32:28)
75. How many sons did Jacob have? (Genesis 35:22)
76. Which of his sons was Jacob's favorite? (Genesis 37:3)
77. What did Jacob give to Joseph? (Genesis 37:3)
78. Why did Joseph's brothers hate him? (Genesis 37:4)
79. What did the brothers do to Joseph? (Genesis 37:28)

80. Where was Joseph taken? (Genesis 37:36)
81. To whom did the slave traders sell Joseph? (Genesis 37:36)
82. Who helped Joseph while he was in prison? (Genesis 39:21)
83. What did Joseph do for two prisoners? (Genesis 40)
84. Why did Pharaoh want to see Joseph? (Genesis 41:15)
85. What did Joseph tell Pharaoh about his dreams? (Genesis 41:16)
86. Tell what the Pharaoh's dreams were about. (Genesis 41:17-24)
87. Tell what Pharaoh's dreams meant. (Genesis 41:26-31)
88. Whom did Pharaoh put in charge of Joseph's plan? (Genesis 41:39, 40)
89. What did Joseph do to prepare for the famine? (Genesis 41:48)
90. What did Joseph do with the grain when the famine came? (Genesis 41:56)
91. Why did Joseph's brothers come to Egypt? (Genesis 42:3)
92. What reminded Joseph of the dreams he had when he was a boy? (Genesis 37:5-8; 42:6)
93. Which brother did Joseph keep in Egypt when the brothers returned home? (Genesis 42:24)
94. Whom did Joseph command them to bring back with them? (Genesis 42:20)
95. What did the brothers find in their sacks when they opened them? (Genesis 42:27)
96. Why didn't Jacob want to send Benjamin to Egypt? (Genesis 42:38)
97. Why did Jacob finally let Benjamin go to Egypt? (Genesis 43:1)
98. What did they find in one sack when they left for home the second time? (Genesis 44:12)
99. Which of the brothers wanted to stay as a slave in the place of Benjamin? (Genesis 44:18)
100. What did Pharaoh do for Joseph's family? (Genesis 45:18)
101. What were the names of Joseph's two sons? (Genesis 48:1)
102. What land did Pharaoh give to Joseph's family in Egypt? (Genesis 47:27)
103. What did the new Pharaoh think of the Israelite nation? (Exodus 1:9)
104. What did he do to the Israelites? (Exodus 1:11)
105. What did Pharaoh command the people to do with all the Israelite boy babies? (Exodus 1:22)
106. How did Moses' mother hide him from Pharaoh? (Exodus 2:3)
107. Who watched over the baby while he floated on the river? (Exodus 2:4)
108. What was the name of Moses' sister? (Exodus 15:21)
109. What was the name of Moses' brother? (Exodus 4:14)
110. Who found the basket with a baby in it? (Exodus 2:5)
111. What did the princess do with the baby? (Exodus 2:10)
112. Who was the lady the princess found to take care of the baby? (Exodus 2:8)
113. Why did Pharaoh get angry with Moses? (Exodus 2:11, 12)
114. Why did Moses run away from Egypt? (Exodus 2:15)
115. Where did Moses go? (Exodus 2:15)
116. What did Moses do when he was in Midian? (Exodus 3:1)
117. How did the Lord appear to Moses on the mountainside of Horeb? (Exodus 3:2)

118. Why did God tell Moses to take off his shoes? (Exodus 3:5)
119. Where did God want Moses to go? (Exodus 3:10)
120. What did God want Moses to do? (Exodus 3:10)
121. Why didn't Moses want to go back to Egypt? (Exodus 3:11)
122. How was Moses going to be able to prove to the Israelites that he was sent from God? (Exodus 4:1-9)
123. Whom did God send with Moses to help him? (Exodus 4:14)
124. What were the signs God gave to Moses? (Exodus 4:2-7)
125. Why didn't Pharaoh want to let the people go? (Exodus 5:5)
126. What did Pharaoh do to the people of Israel after Moses asked for them to leave Egypt? (Exodus 5:10, 11)
127. What miracle did Moses do when he first went to Pharaoh? (Exodus 7:10)
128. What was the last plague? (Exodus 11:1-5)
129. What did the magicians of Pharaoh finally say about the miracles? (Exodus 8:19)
130. Why did Pharaoh finally let the people of Israel go? (Exodus 11:5)
131. How did the Israelites know that God was leading them? (Exodus 14:19)
132. Whose body did the people of Israel take out of Egypt with them? (Exodus 13:19)
133. What was a Nazarite? (Judges 13:5)
134. What two things was Sampson not allowed to do? (Judges 13:4)
135. Where did Sampson go to get a wife? (Judges 14:2)
136. Where did Sampson find the honey? (Judges 14:8)
137. What did Sampson tell at his wedding feast? (Judges 14:12)
138. What did Sampson do to the Philistine cornfields? (Judges 15:4, 5)
139. What did Sampson do to the people of Gaza? (Judges 16:3)
140. What was the name of the Philistine woman that Sampson loved? (Judges 16:4)
141. What did the Philistines want Delilah to do? (Judges 16:5)
142. Why did Sampson finally tell Delilah his secret? (Judges 16:16)
143. How was Sampson captured? (Judges 16:19)
144. What did the Philistines do to Sampson? (Judges 16:21)
145. How did Sampson die? (Judges 16:29, 30)
146. What did Hannah want more than anything? (1 Samuel 1:11)
147. What was the name of the prophet in the temple where Hannah prayed? (1 Samuel 1:9)
148. What was the child named? (1 Samuel 1:20)
149. Why did Hannah take Samuel to the temple to live? (1 Samuel 1:27, 28)
150. What did Hannah bring to Samuel every year? (1 Samuel 2:19)
151. When did the Lord speak to Samuel? (1 Samuel 3:3, 4)
152. Who told Samuel that it was the Lord calling him? (1 Samuel 3:9)
153. What did the people of Israel ask Samuel to give them? (1 Samuel 8:5)
154. Why did they want a king? (1 Samuel 8:5)
155. Who told Samuel to give them a king? (1 Samuel 8:7)
156. For what was Saul looking when he met Samuel? (1 Samuel 9:3)
157. How did Samuel know that Saul was coming? (1 Samuel 9:15, 16)
158. To which tribe did Saul belong? (1 Samuel 9:21)

159. Who anointed Saul to be Israel's king? (1 Samuel 10:1)
160. How did Saul disobey God? (1 Samuel 15:9)
161. What was Saul's punishment? (1 Samuel 15:26)
162. Who did King Saul try to blame for his sin? (1 Samuel 15:21)
163. How did Samuel know that Saul had sinned? (1 Samuel 15:16)
164. Where did God send Samuel to find a new king? (1 Samuel 16:1)
165. Why was Samuel afraid to go? (1 Samuel 16:2)
166. How many sons did Jesse have? (1 Samuel 16:10, 11)
167. Which son had God chosen to be king? (1 Samuel 16:13)
168. What work did David do for his father? (1 Samuel 16:11)
169. What happened to King Saul after he disobeyed God? (1 Samuel 16:14)
170. What helped King Saul when he was troubled? (1 Samuel 16:16)
171. Who was brought to the palace to play the harp for the king? (1 Samuel 16:18, 19)
172. With what nation were the Israelites at war? (1 Samuel 17:1)
173. What was the name of the giant Philistine? (1 Samuel 17:4)
174. What did Goliath do every morning at the battlefield? (1 Samuel 17:8)
175. Why didn't Saul and his soldiers fight the giant? (1 Samuel 17:11)
176. How did David know God would give him strength? (1 Samuel 17:37)
177. What did David want to do? (1 Samuel 17:32)
178. How did David kill the giant? (1 Samuel 17:49, 50)
179. What was the name of the young prince who became friends with David? (1 Samuel 18:1)
180. Why did Saul become jealous of David? (1 Samuel 7, 8)
181. How did Saul try to kill David? (1 Samuel 19:10)
182. How did Jonathan warn David that Saul was trying to kill him? (1 Samuel 20:20-22)
183. What did David and Jonathan promise to one another? (1 Samuel 20:42)
184. Where did David live while he was hiding from Saul? (1 Samuel 22:1)
185. Why didn't David kill Saul in the cave when he had a chance? (1 Samuel 24:6)
186. What did David do the night he went into Saul's camp while everyone was asleep? (1 Samuel 26:12)
187. How did Saul die? (1 Samuel 31:4)
188. Who died the same day Saul died? (1 Samuel 31:2)
189. What city was called the city of David? (2 Samuel 5:6)
190. What did David bring to Jerusalem? (2 Samuel 6:12)
191. What was the name of Jonathan's son? (2 Samuel 9:6)
192. How did Mephibosheth become crippled? (2 Samuel 4:4)
193. Why did David send for Jonathan's son? (2 Samuel 9:3)
194. What did David do for Mephibosheth? (2 Samuel 9:7)
195. Who became king of Israel after David? (1 Kings 2:12)
196. What did Solomon ask God to give him? (1 Kings 3:9)
197. Why couldn't David build God's house? (1 Kings 5:3)
198. Where did Solomon get the cedar trees to build the temple? (1 Kings 5:6)
199. How long did it take to build God's house? (1 Kings 6:38)
200. Who came to dedicate the building? (1 Kings 8:1)
201. How did God show His presence in the temple? (1 Kings 8:10)

202. What was the name of Ahab's wife? (1 Kings 16:31)
203. What did Elijah tell King Ahab? (1 Kings 17:1)
204. Who told Elijah to hide? (1 Kings 17:2, 3)
205. How did God care for Elijah while he hid at the brook? (1 Kings 17:6)
206. Where did Elijah go when the brook dried up? (1 Kings 17:9)
207. What did Elijah ask the widow to do for him? (1 Kings 17:11)
208. What did the widow tell Elijah? (1 Kings 17:12)
209. How did God care for Elijah and the widow? (1 Kings 17:16)
210. What happened to the widow's son? (1 Kings 17:17)
211. When God heard Elijah pray for the widow's son, what did He do? (1 Kings 17:22)
212. How many years passed before it rained? (1 Kings 18:1)
213. Where did Elijah and the prophets of Baal hold their contest? (1 Kings 18:19)
214. How many times did Elijah ask God to send rain? (1 Kings 18:44)
215. What was the name of the king who conquered Jerusalem when Daniel was a boy? (Daniel 1:1)
216. What did Daniel refuse to do? (Daniel 1:8)
217. What was the test Daniel proposed to the steward? (Daniel 1:12)
218. What happened at the end of the ten days? (Daniel 1:15)
219. How did Daniel and his friends do when the king examined them? (Daniel 1:20)
220. What did the king want his wise men to tell him? (Daniel 2:3)
221. Why did the king say he was going to kill all the wise men? (Daniel 2:7-12)
222. Who asked the king for more time? (Daniel 2:6)
223. Who told Daniel what the dream was about and what it meant? (Daniel 2:19)
224. What did the king do for Daniel after he told him about the dream? (Daniel 2:48)
225. What were the names of Daniel's three friends? (Daniel 2:49)
226. What did King Nebuchadnezzar want the people of his kingdom to do? (Daniel 3:5)
227. Who would not worship the idol? (Daniel 3:12)
228. What did the king do to Shadrach, Meshach, and Abednego? (Daniel 3:20)
229. What happened to the men who threw Shadrach, Meshach, and Abednego into the fiery furnace? (Daniel 3:22)
230. Whom did the king see walking in the furnace with the three men? (Daniel 3:25)
231. What did the king think about the God of Israel after this? (Daniel 3:29)
232. What job did King Darius give to Daniel? (Daniel 6:2)
233. What did the other government officials try to do to Daniel? (Daniel 6:4)
234. What did the other government officials get King Darius to do? (Daniel 6:7)
235. What did Daniel do after the law was passed? (Daniel 6:10)
236. Did the king want to punish Daniel? (Daniel 6:14)
237. What did the king do to Daniel? (Daniel 6:16)
238. How did God show His love and care to Daniel? (Daniel 6:22)

239. What kind of work did Zechariah do? (Luke 1:5)
240. What was the name of Zechariah's wife? (Luke 1:5)
241. What unusual happening occurred while Zechariah was in the temple? (Luke 1:11)
242. What did the angel tell Zechariah? (Luke 1:13)
243. Why didn't Zechariah believe the angel? (Luke 1:18)
244. What was the name of the angel? (Luke 1:19)
245. What sign was Zechariah given? (Luke 1:20)
246. What did all the relatives want to name the baby? (Luke 1:59)
247. How did Zechariah tell the relatives the name of the baby? (Luke 1:63)
248. What happened to Zechariah after the baby was named? (Luke 1:64)
249. What was the name of the girl in Nazareth who was visited by an angel? (Luke 1:26, 27)
250. To whom was the girl engaged? (Luke 1:27)
251. What did the angel tell Mary? (Luke 1:31-33)
252. What other child did the angel tell Mary about? (Luke 1:36)
253. Whom did Mary go to visit? (Luke 1:40)
254. What did the angel tell Joseph? (Matthew 1:20, 21)
255. Why did Mary and Joseph go to Bethlehem? (Luke 2:3)
256. Why did Mary and Joseph spend the night in the stable? (Luke 2:7)
257. What happened that night in the stable? (Luke 2:7)
258. What did the shepherds in the fields see that night? (Luke 2:9)
259. What did the angels tell the shepherds? (Luke 2:11)
260. What did the shepherds do after the angels left? (Luke 2:15, 16)
261. Why did the Wise-men come to Jerusalem? (Matthew 2:2)
262. What three gifts did the Wise-men bring? (Matthew 2:11)
263. Why didn't the Wise-men report back to Herod? (Matthew 2:12)
264. What did the angel tell Joseph in a dream? (Matthew 2:13)
265. What did Herod do when the Wise-men didn't return? (Matthew 2:16)
266. After Herod died, Joseph took his family to live in what city? (Matthew 2:23)
267. Where did Joseph take his family the year Jesus was twelve years old? (Luke 2:42)
268. What did Mary and Joseph discover when they started home? (Luke 2:43)
269. Where did they find Jesus? (Luke 2:46)
270. What was Jesus doing when they found Him? (Luke 2:46)
271. What was the name of the river where John the Baptist baptized people? (Luke 3:3)
272. Who baptized Jesus? (Matthew 3:13-17)
273. What miraculous thing happened when Jesus was baptized? (Luke 3:22)
274. How old was Jesus when He began His ministry? (Luke 3:23)
275. How long did Jesus stay in the wilderness without food? (Luke 4:2)
276. What did the devil want Jesus to do in order to get bread when He was hungry? (Luke 4:3)
277. Why did the devil take Jesus to a high mountain? (Luke 4:5)
278. What did the devil promise to give Jesus if Jesus would worship him? (Luke 4:6)

279. How did Jesus answer the devil? (Luke 4:8)
280. What did Jesus begin to do after He came back from the wilderness? (Luke 4:15)
281. Why did John's disciples follow Jesus? (John 1:35-37)
282. Who were the two men that Jesus promised to make fishers of men? (Matthew 4:18)
283. Who were the sons of Zebedee who went with Jesus? (Matthew 4:21)
284. What new name did Jesus give to Simon? (Mark 3:16)
285. Whom did Philip bring to Jesus? (John 1:45)
286. What happened at Cana? (John 2:1)
287. What did Mary, Jesus' mother, tell the servants to do? (John 2:5)
288. What did Jesus tell the servants to do? (John 2:7)
289. What happened to the water? (John 2:9)
290. What did the governor say about the wine made from water? (John 2:10)
291. What did Jesus send Peter and John to do? (Luke 22:8)
292. How were Peter and John to find a room? (Luke 22:10-12)
293. What did Jesus do for the disciples before the supper? (John 13:5)
294. Why did Jesus wash their feet? (John 13:14, 15)
295. What did Jesus do with the bread and cup? (Mark 14:22)
296. Who betrayed Jesus? (John 13:26)
297. How much money did Judas get for betraying Jesus? (Matthew 26:15)
298. Why did Jesus go to the Garden of Gethsemane? (Matthew 26:39)
299. Who went with Jesus? (Mark 14:33)
300. What sign did Judas give to the Jewish leaders? (Mark 14:44)
301. Who tried to defend Jesus? (John 18:10)
302. Who claimed he didn't know Jesus? (Mark 14:70, 71)
303. To which ruler was Jesus taken? (Mark 15:1)
304. What did Pilate ask Jesus? (Mark 15:2)
305. How did Jesus answer His accusers? (Mark 15:3)
306. Who did the Jews want set free instead of Jesus? (Mark 15:11)
307. What did the Roman soldiers put on Jesus' head? (John 19:2)
308. How did the Roman soldiers treat Jesus? (John 19:3)
309. What was the name of the hill where Jesus was crucified? (John 19:17)
310. How many were crucified that day? (John 19:18)
311. What was on the sign Pilate ordered nailed to Jesus' cross? (John 19:19)
312. What did the soldiers do with Jesus' clothing? (John 19:23, 24)
313. What did one of the thieves ask Jesus to do? (Luke 23:42)
314. What was Jesus' answer? (Luke 23:43)
315. Who received permission to remove Jesus from the cross? (John 19:38)
316. Who came to visit the tomb? (John 20:1)
317. What did Mary Magdalene do when she saw the tomb was empty? (John 20:2)
318. What did the angels tell the women at the tomb? (Mark 16:6)
319. How do we know Saul was a Roman citizen? (Acts 16:37)
320. What did Saul have to do with the stoning of Stephen? (Acts 7:58)
321. What did Saul do to the Christians? (Acts 9:1)
322. Why did Saul ask for a letter addressed to the synagogues in Damascus? (Acts 9:2)

323. Why was Saul going to Damascus? (Acts 9:2)
324. What did Saul see on the road to Damascus? (Acts 9:3)
325. What did Saul hear on the road to Damascus? (Acts 9:4)
326. Who was speaking to Saul? (Acts 9:5)
327. What was wrong with Saul after the light was gone? (Acts 9:9)
328. How long did Saul go without food and water? (Acts 9:9)
329. Where did Saul go after his vision? (Acts 9:8)
330. What was the name of the believer the Lord spoke to in Damascus about Saul? (Acts 9:10)
331. Where did the Lord tell Ananias to go? (Acts 9:11)
332. Whom did the Lord tell Ananias to ask for? (Acts 9:11)
333. Why didn't Ananias want to go? (Acts 9:13)
334. Why did the Lord want Ananias to help Saul? (Acts 9:15)
335. What did Saul do as soon as he could see? (Acts 9:18)
336. What did the Lord help Ananias do for Saul? (Acts 9:17)
337. What did Saul immediately begin to tell everyone? (Acts 9:20)
338. Why did the Jews in Damascus want to kill Saul? (Acts 9:22, 23)
339. How did Saul manage to escape the Jews in Damascus? (Acts 9:25)
340. Who helped the believers in Jerusalem accept Saul? (Acts 9:26, 27)
341. What did Peter do for Aeneas, who had been paralyzed for eight years? (Acts 9:34)
342. In whose name did Peter heal Aeneas? (Acts 9:34)
343. Who was the lady from Joppa who was always doing kind things for the poor? (Acts 9:36)
344. When Dorcas died, what did her friends do? (Acts 9:38)
345. What were the widows of Joppa doing when Peter arrived? (Acts 9:39)
346. What did Peter do by Dorcas' bedside? (Acts 9:40)
347. What happened to Dorcas after Peter prayed? (Acts 9:41)
348. Where did Peter stay while he was in Joppa? (Acts 9:43)
349. What was the name of the Roman army officer who lived in Caesarea? (Acts 10:1)
350. What did Cornelius see one afternoon about three? (Acts 10:3)
351. What did the angel tell Cornelius to do? (Acts 10:5)
352. What did Cornelius do as soon as the angel left? (Acts 10:7, 8)
353. Why did Peter go up on the roof of the house? (Acts 10:9)
354. Describe the vision Peter had. (Acts 10:11-13)
355. How many times did Peter see the vision? (Acts 10:16)
356. What did the Holy Spirit tell Peter about the three men from Caesarea? (Acts 10:19, 20)
357. Why did Peter tell Cornelius to stand up? (Acts 10:26)
358. What did Peter learn from his vision? (Acts 10:34)
359. What message did Peter tell Cornelius? (Acts 10:34-43)
360. What happened to Cornelius that day? (Acts 10:48)
361. Why did Barnabas go looking for Saul? (Acts 11:26)
362. Where were the believers first called Christians? (Acts 11:26)
363. Why did the believers at Antioch send Saul and Barnabas to Jerusalem? (Acts 11:29, 30)
364. Who were the first missionaries? (Acts 13:1-3)